History on the Run

written by Mary Kaiser Donev • illustrated by Robert Casilla

 Macmillan
McGraw-Hill

New York   Farmington

Dear Diary,

I'm riding from St. Louis, Missouri to Los Angeles, California to see my Grandma and Grandpa. My Uncle Fred is taking me. He's a conductor on the train.

I didn't really want to come. I just wanted to stay home this summer, hang out with my friends, do nothing, and watch TV.

Mom said I'd have fun. She took the same trip with Uncle Fred when she was young. And Uncle Fred said I could help him do his chores, like collecting tickets and calling out the stops. So I decided to come.

The train is long with fifteen passenger cars and ten or more freight cars, too. And it's about to take off now. Here comes Uncle Fred.

More later, Diary.

Dear Diary,

Uncle Fred is funny! When we collected the tickets, he made all the kids laugh by making faces at them. He told everybody I was his new helper.

Uncle Fred took me to meet the engineer who drives the train. It was fun. She even let me blow the whistle.

Uncle Fred told me he loves train travel because he likes to feel the gentle rocking of the car as it moves along the tracks. And he likes what he sees out the window.

I asked him, what was so interesting out the window? It's just trees and rocks and stuff like that.

Uncle Fred almost shouted, "History, Amy! History!"

He explained that the train is following the old Santa Fe Trail. That's the route that Native Americans first made many years ago through the mountains in the Southwest. Later settlers followed the same trail. But their covered wagons were not as comfortable as this train.

Tomorrow we go through Dodge City, Kansas. Uncle Fred calls it the cowboy capital of the world. It was the home of some of the roughest, toughest cowboys. It was a wild place full of people who shot first and asked questions later.

Uncle Fred told me about one of the people who helped clean up the town. His name was Wyatt Earp. But he was rough, too, and he used guns. Sometimes he wasn't much better than the outlaws. One time he loaded his gun, put it in his pocket and shot a hole through his own coat!

Uncle Fred told me that so many buffalo were killed outside Dodge City that they used the bones as money at the banks there.

Maybe it will be interesting to see Dodge City after all.

Uncle Fred says he knows lots of cool stuff about places we're traveling through. He promised to tell me more tomorrow.

I have my own private room on the train with a bed to sleep in that folds down out of the wall. Right now, it's late and I'm going to try out my bed. Uncle Fred said the clackety-clack of the train wheels would sing me to sleep. Good night, Diary!

Dear Diary,

After riding through a little corner of Colorado today, we went through Raton, New Mexico. We were more than 6,000 feet above sea level. It was really high up and a little scary but the train made it through okay.

Uncle Fred told me a man named Dick Wootton once built 27 miles of road over the pass in the mountains. He charged people $1.50 to bring horses and wagons over his road. He made so much money that he brought barrels full of silver dollars to the bank!

Some of the oldest apartment complexes in the world are in New Mexico. They're called pueblos and they were built by Native Americans more than five hundred years ago. Uncle Fred told me some of those sandstone and mud buildings are still standing and people can visit them.

When we went through Winslow, Arizona, Uncle Fred said we were near an enormous hole called a crater that's more than two miles wide. Astronauts once trained there so they could practice before they walked on the moon.

This really surprised me! Uncle Fred said more than 140 years ago the U.S. Army brought camels from the Middle East by boat to Texas and then across land to Arizona. The Army wanted to use the camels in the American desert.

The camels were kept below deck. One camel was so tall, people had to cut a hole in the deck so his hump would fit!

When the camels were taken off the boat they were so excited that they jumped all about. Texans had never seen camels before. They were so scared that they all ran away from the camels!

The camels didn't work out for the Army for many reasons. One is that no one wanted to ride them. People thought they were mean animals and not easy to train. So the camels were set free. And for years afterward people saw the wild camels roaming the American desert.

Got to go now, Diary. Uncle Fred's going to need me to collect tickets at Flagstaff. That's near the Grand Canyon. I'll write more later before I go to bed.

Dear Diary,

Tomorrow morning we'll be in Los Angeles. We'll be traveling through the desert tonight and I'm glad I don't have to walk. Uncle Fred said it can get up to 120 degrees sometimes!

I bet Uncle Fred he couldn't find anything interesting in the desert. After all, everything is dead there.

"Not true," said Uncle Fred. "The desert has lots of plants and animals. But what interests me the most is the dead stuff!"

He said that one of the oldest prehistoric tool sites in this part of the world is in the desert in Barstow, California. Scientists have found thousands of tools that people used long ago for things like scraping meat off bones. They don't just pull the tools out of the ground, either. They move the dirt away gently with tooth brushes and dental instruments like my dentist uses to clean my teeth.

The tools they found are more than 200,000 years old. When Uncle Fred said that was older than he is, I laughed and said that was pretty old!

Uncle Fred said it isn't as old as the rock they have in Barstow. It's a meteorite that weighs nearly three tons. They call it the Old Woman. It dropped from some distant place in the universe many years ago. It's the second largest meteorite ever found in the U.S. and it weighs almost as much as an elephant.

I told Uncle Fred that I was sad that the trip would be over tomorrow and that I won't be able to hear any more of his stories. He said any time I want to come back and ride the rails with him, I can.

So, Diary, where would you like to go by train next summer? It's more fun than staying at home, doing nothing, and watching TV!